Protecting Your Assets in The Pandemic Age

How to Safeguard Your Assets from Creditors, the Government, and Other Predators

Pierre Mouchette

Real Property Experts LLC

Copyright © 2020 by Pierre Mouchette
All rights reserved. No part of this publication may be reproduced or used in any manner without written permission of the Copyright Holder, except by a reviewer who may quote brief passages in a review.

First Edition: November 2020
Real Property Experts LLC
Web Address: https://www.rpe4u.com
Contact: publications@rpe4u.com

Note: This publication comes in a variety of formats, such as Paperback Book | Print-on-Demand (POD) and Electronic Book (e-books). Some material included with the paperback versions of this book may not be included in e-books, and vice versa.

Disclaimer: This Real Property Experts LLC (RPE) publication provides information about the subject matter covered. The author and publisher of this content are not acting as licensed professionals in the presentation of covered material and are not qualified to give advice normally provided by professionals in the fields of expertise of this content, nor are they responsible for errors and omissions. The information and statements made, are for educational purposes and are not intended to replace a one-on-one relationship with a qualified attorney, accountant, tax professional, or other licensed professionals. You are solely responsible for the use of any content and hold Real Property Experts LLC, its' subsidiary's and members harmless in any event or claim, demand, or damage, including reasonable attorneys' fees, asserted by any third party or arising out of your use of, or conduct on, articles and/or products.

RPE writers provide applicable content and break down complex topics so they are easier to understand. Information given may not apply to your specific situation, and products or services recommended may not be a good fit for your application. While RPE strives to provide accurate up-to-date content, we cannot guarantee the accuracy and completeness of information provided. By using this content, you understand that all material is an expression of opinions and not professional advice.

RPE regularly updates articles, but it is possible that we may miss something. Use our content as a starting point before selecting to use and choose a service or product. The reader is advised to keep up to date on activities in their locale by consulting with the appropriate licensed professionals for decisions that could affect them

PREFACE

The reason for writing **Protecting Your Assets in The Pandemic Age** is that COVID-19, has affected so many people in so many ways. An article on CNN 10/15/20 stated **"Covid-19 deaths will rise almost 80% by February** (2021), **researchers foresee."** The current statistics are staggering, and worldwide astronomical. Yes, many families have been affected by the pandemic, and if not, you know someone who has been affected.

The book's purpose is to provide information to those who in their wisdom **PLAN, PREPARE, MANAGE, and IMPLEMENT** for themselves and family.

"By failing to prepare, you are preparing to fail." .... *Benjamin Franklin*

For comments on this publication please write to us at REAL PROPERTY EXPERTS. Stay safe, well, and healthy.

Pierre Mouchette, Author
pierre@rpe4u.com

SPECIAL FEATURES

THE SYNCHRONICITY INVESTOR (https://www.synchronicity-investor.com) provides world class solutions for all. THE SYNCHRONICITY INVESTOR (TSI) is committed to providing you with the information that you need to make informed decisions. We encourage you to think of THE SYNCHRONICITY INVESTOR as your go to source for knowledgeable information. Additionally, on the website you can:

- Keep up to date – when there are important changes to our publications, we will post updates online.
- Publications – the website contains hundreds of articles on everyday issues, all published by Real Property Experts and available for free. There you will find more Books, Booklets, How-to-Articles, Guides and much, much more.
- Also, while visiting the website, be sure to stop at the TSI-Digital Desk. There you will find many items of interest!

Contents

CHAPTER 1   IN THE BEGINNING ....- 7 -
    The Mission ....- 8 -
  TEAM MEMBER CLARIFICATION..- 11 -
CHAPTER 2   PROBATE, PLANNING and TOOLS.......................................- 12 -
    PROBATE..- 13 -
      What Happens to An Estate After You Die? ....- 13 -
      What Is Probate?..- 13 -
      Who Handles the Estate? ....- 13 -
    WHAT IS A WILL ....- 14 -
    ABOUT WILLS...- 14 -
      Does the Will Give Authority to Sell Property?...- 14 -
      Can A House Be Sold While in Probate? ....- 14 -
    WHAT IS ESTATE PLANNING?...- 15 -
      Probate Planning and Probate Avoidance ....- 15 -
      Tax and Financial Planning..- 15 -
      Estate Taxes ....- 16 -
      Inheritance Taxes...- 16 -
    ESTATE PLANNING TOOLS ....- 17 -
      The Last Will and Testament..- 17 -
      Trusts ....- 17 -
      Transfer-on-Death Assets ....- 18 -
    WHAT DOES ESTATE PLANNING CONSIST OF?.................................- 19 -
      Estate Planning Trusts ....- 20 -
      Elder Care Planning Trusts ....- 21 -
      Estate Tax Planning Trusts ....- 22 -
    THE IRA TRUST ....- 25 -
      Asset and Other Protection for Your Beneficiaries...................................- 25 -
      IRA Hitches ....- 26 -
      Planning for a Blended Family ....- 26 -

MORE TRUSTS?...	- 27 -
CHAPTER 3 PLANNING FOR INCAPACITIES	- 28 -
PLANNING FOR INCAPACITIES	- 29 -
Powers of Attorney and Medical Directives...............................	- 29 -
Advance Medical Directives	- 30 -
CHAPTER 4 SELECTING YOUR ATTORNEY	- 31 -
BUYER BEWARE	- 32 -
Estate Planning Tips	- 32 -
Questions for A Potential Trust and Estate Planning Attorney..	- 33 -
APPENDIX - A	- 35 -
Glossary	- 36 -
FYI - CLARIFICATIONS	- 39 -
Parties To, And Their Functions in The Probate Process............	- 40 -
APPENDIX - B	- 41 -
Benefits of Creating an Itemized Asset List	- 42 -
Personal Information	- 42 -
Creating Your List..	- 42 -
Inventory List	- 42 -

CHAPTER 1   IN THE BEGINNING

In this age of insecurity about what to expect next, as the tabloids and live news coverage exploit the daily upsurge of COVID-19 statistics, one can only in good conscious **PLAN, PREPARE, MANAGE, and IMPLEMENT** methods to protect themselves and family.

The Mission

Key to the mission of protecting self and family is having a plan. From this plan you will be able to organize the mission and finalize it with your professional team. Segments to this mission are:

The Plan - the following are items recommended for the preparation of securing your family's future:

- **Inventory** - besides the outline of wants and needs prepared by you and your spouse, you should make a detailed list of all your current assets and their value. To do this make a list of all valuable items in your home, both inside and outside.
  Note: add notes if someone comes to mind to whom you would like to give items to after death.

  - **Non-Physical Assets** - things that are owned on paper or other entitlements that are predicated on your death. Items listed here could include brokerage accounts, 401(k) plans, IRAs, bank accounts, life insurance policies, long-term care policies, homeowners, auto, disability, and health insurances.

    When making this list, include all account numbers and list the location of any physical documents you have in your possession. You may also want to list contact information for the companies or businesses holding these non-physical possessions.

    Note: If you have changed jobs over the years, it is likely that you may have several different 401(k) retirement plans still open with past employers or even several different IRA accounts. You may want to consider consolidating these accounts into one individual IRA. Consolidating accounts allows for better investment choices, lower costs, a larger selection of investments, less paperwork, and easier management.

  - **Liabilities and Obligations List** - make a list of open credit cards and other obligations that you have. This should include auto loans, mortgages, home equity lines of credit (HELOCs), and any other debts you might owe. Again, include account numbers, the location of signed agreements, and the contact information of the companies or businesses holding the debt.

- **Memberships List** - any organizations that you belong to should also be listed. In some cases, these organizations may have accidental life insurance benefits (at no cost) on their members and your estate may be eligible to collect. These organizations might include AARP, The American Legion, and professional accreditation associations.

After completing the above, we recommend:

- **Review Your Retirement Accounts** – all accounts and policies that have designated beneficiaries will pass directly to those people or entities upon your death. It does not matter how you direct these accounts or policies be distributed in your will or trust, because the beneficiary designations associated with the account will take precedence. Review each of these accounts to verify that the beneficiaries are current and listed exactly as wanted. This is especially important if you have divorced and remarried.

- **Update Your Insurance** - all retirement accounts, life insurance and annuities will pass directly to beneficiaries. It is important to contact all life insurance companies where you maintain policies to ensure that your beneficiaries are up-to-date and listed correctly.

- **Assign Transfer on Death Designations** - assets bequeathed in a will often go through probate, as do assets if someone dies intestate. The process, in which your assets are distributed per court instruction (PROBATE), can be costly and time-consuming. However, many accounts such as bank savings, CD accounts, and individual brokerage accounts are unnecessarily probated every day. If you have these accounts, they can be set up or amended, to have a **Transfer on Death (TOD)** designation, which lets beneficiaries receive assets without going through the probate process. Contact your custodian or bank to set up **TOD** on your accounts.

- **Select a Responsible Executor** - your **Executor** will oversee administering your Will when you die. It is important that you select an individual who is responsible and in a good mental state to make decisions. Do not immediately assume that your spouse is the best choice. Think about how emotions related to your death will affect this person's decision-making ability. If you foresee an issue, consider other qualified individuals.

Note: when your lists are completed, you should incorporate any last-minute changes, make copies for both you, your spouse, accountant, and if you have, your financial advisor, and tax professional.

To Prepare – here again, incorporate any suggestions from those that you provided information to under the planning stage. Now it is time to organize a list of potential team members. This team will vary depending on your age, responsibilities, and assets. Some team members may include:

- Executor
- Certified Public Accountant (CPA)
- Financial Advisor
- Tax Professional
- Attorney or preferably a Trust and Estate Planning Attorney
- Any other professionals that you deem necessary

To Implement – after the final review with your **Attorney | Trust and Estate Planning Attorney** and the revisions thereto, you should distribute copies of the documentation to:

- The original should be retained by your **Attorney | Trust and Estate Planning Attorney** (highly recommended as you will understand in reading CHAPTER 2).

- Provide copies of the same to your Team members.

- A copy should be given to your spouse (if married) and placed in a safe deposit box.

- Keep a copy for yourself in a safe place.

Note: only the original Will, the "wet signature" document, in estate-planning lingo, can be filed for probate.

To Manage – keep all paperwork and documents up to date. If there are any changes in your life notify all Team members, make modifications to your policies and other documents with the changes being incorporated through your **Attorney |Trust and Estate Planning Attorney.** Redistribute the appropriate documents to all Team members.

TEAM MEMBER CLARIFICATION

Certified Public Accountants (CPAs) - is an accounting professional licensed and credentialed by a state or territory to offer accounting services, including tax preparation, to the public. A CPA keeps or inspects financial records to ensure that the information they represent is accurate and complies with relevant laws and regulations. This can include:

- Examining financial statements to ensure they are accurate.
- Prepares tax returns.
- Provides financial forecasts.
- Provides auditing services.

Enrolled agents (EAs) – these are tax professionals that are authorized to represent taxpayers before the Internal Revenue Service (IRS). These agents have unlimited practice rights, meaning that they can represent any taxpayer (individual, business, or organization), and are authorized by the IRS to deal with any federal tax issue.

Enrolled agents' status is the highest level of IRS certification.

Preparer Tax Identification Number (PTIN) – this is a number issued by the IRS to a professional tax preparer, such as Certified Public Accountants and Enrolled Agents. A PTIN is only required for those professionals who accept payment to prepare tax returns.

Note: Federal regulations give unlimited practice rights before the IRS to only three kinds of professionals:

- Lawyers
- Certified Public Accountants (CPAs)
- Enrolled Agents (EAs)

CHAPTER 2   PROBATE, PLANNING and TOOLS

PROBATE

What Happens to An Estate After You Die?
Everything you own at the time of your death becomes your estate. Then, the estate goes through the **Probate** process, where a **Probate Court** decides what happens to your assets.

If you have a Will, the court uses it as their guide. If you do not have a Will or if it was invalid for some reason, you are considered to have **died intestate** and the court uses local intestacy laws to decide who inherits your (assets) **estate.**

What Is Probate?
Probate is the process of verifying that your Will is legal and that your final wishes are carried out. A Will does not help your estate avoid probate. It simply makes the process smoother because the court can use it as a guide to what you wanted.

For most **'small estates,'** probate is a simple process that can be completed (6 to 9 months) quickly. However, things may slow down if someone contests the Will, which means they challenge what is in it. Contesting a will can prolong the probate process for months and potentially cost a lot in lawyer and or court fees.

If there is no Will, the estate still goes through the **Probate Court.** The difference is that a **Probate Judge** will appoint someone to handle the disbursing of assets.

Who Handles the Estate?
Ideally, you have created a Will that names someone as your **Executor.** The **Executor** of your estate manages your estate through the probate process. They handle tax bills, debts you had not paid off, and other matters affecting your estate. The **Executor** also oversees the disbursement of your assets to beneficiaries.

If you do not name an **Executor** before you die, the **Probate Judge** will choose an **Estate Administrator.**

WHAT IS A WILL

A Will is a legal document created to provide instructions on how an individual's property and custody of minor children if any, should be handled after death. The individual expresses their wishes through this document and names an **Executor** that they trust to fulfill the stated intentions.

The authenticity of a Will is determined through a legal process known as **probate.** Probate is the first step taken in administering to the estate of a deceased person and distributing assets to the beneficiaries. When an individual dies, the custodian of the Will must take the Will to the **Probate Court** or to the **Executor** named in the Will within 30 days of the death of the **Testator.**

During the probate process the authenticity of the Will is proven to be valid and accepted as the true last testament of the deceased. The court officially appoints the **Executor** named in the Will, which in turn gives the executor the legal power to act on behalf of the deceased.

ABOUT WILLS

Does the Will Give Authority to Sell Property?
Once the decedent's Will is authenticated by the probate court, if the Will authorizes the sale of real or personal property, the Executor | Administrator need not seek court approval for the sale, for any reason without limitation if it is in the best interest of the estate. If the Will places limitations on the power of sale, those limitations will remain in effect. If the Will has not authorized the sale of the estate property, they may still do so by getting the permission of the probate court.

Can A House Be Sold While in Probate?
Absolutely! You will need to be the Executor | Administrator of the estate. The money received will go towards the estate's debts, and then divided between the beneficiaries. The sale must be approved by the court to move forward in the process if the Will does not give authority to sell the property.

WHAT IS ESTATE PLANNING?

Estate planning is the term given to the process people go through to prepare for the legal, financial, and personal realities of their death, while an estate plan is a collection of tools specifically designed to address these kinds of issues. Estate planning is not a single topic, but a collection of topics that all involve the practical realities surrounding death and mortality.

Estate planning can be complicated, involving ever-changing considerations, personal preferences, new laws, shifting economic factors, and more. Regardless of age or personal circumstances, creating an estate plan is an essential task for every adult, and understanding what an estate plan is and what specific kinds of issues your plan might address is the first step.

Probate Planning and Probate Avoidance

Probate laws can be complicated, cumbersome, and potentially expensive. Once you die and leave behind an estate, your inheritors cannot receive their inheritances until the probate process is complete. This process involves several steps that must take place. For example, if you left behind any debts, your creditors would have the opportunity to file a claim with the estate. Once filed, the administrator of the estate will have to use estate funds to pay off those debts before he or she can distribute any inheritances.

Today, many estate plans focus on taking probate out of the picture. There are many ways to do this. For example, people who properly create and fund a living trust can effectively make all, or most of their major inheritance transfers completely outside of the probate process. Other probate mitigation tools can include providing lifetime gifts to family and friends, using payable-on-death assets such as life insurance policies, and taking advantage of jointly owned property.

Tax and Financial Planning

A good financial and estate plan can reduce the potential tax burden your estate might one-day face. In some situations, the right plan can allow you to avoid estate, and inheritance taxes completely. However, as with any discussion of tax issues, it is important to note that the current tax laws can and will change in the future. *This is one of the many reasons why talking to an estate planning expert will always be better than trying to craft a plan on your own.*

Estate Taxes

Estate taxes, sometimes referred to as the **'death tax,'** are widely misunderstood by the general population. When you die and leave behind an estate, that estate is worth a certain dollar amount. An estate tax is simply a tax applied to that value.

The estate tax is a tax that you will never have to pay because it only applies after you die. Further, it is not a tax your family or inheritors will have to pay because your estate is responsible for paying it before distributing property as inheritances. If an estate is asset-rich but cash-poor, paying the estate tax may require the liquidation of some assets, to cover the estate tax bill. Further, any time an estate must pay estate taxes, the tax reduces potential inheritances.

The Federal Government has an estate tax, but it does not currently apply unless you leave behind an estate worth more than $11.58 million in 2020. This means that only estates whose values exceed $11.58 million after deductions are made and credits are taken are subject to the federal estate tax on the balance.

In addition to the federal estate tax, some states have enacted state-level estate taxes of their own. These state-level taxes can apply to much smaller estates. Crafting an estate plan that reduces or eliminates any potential state estate tax assessment can be vital if you want to preserve as many of your assets as possible to use for inheritances.

Inheritance Taxes

Like estate taxes, inheritance taxes can apply at both the state and federal level. However, there is no federal inheritance tax, and only a small number of states currently have them on the books.

ESTATE PLANNING TOOLS

The Last Will and Testament

The **Last Will and Testament,** or Will, is the most well-known of estate planning tools. Most people know what a Will is and understand that by making one they can choose what kinds of inheritances they leave behind.

Making a Will is a lot more complicated than just writing your wishes down on a sheet of paper. Every state has specific rules that apply to people who make a Will, and if you fail to follow those rules, your Will is useless. Minimum requirements include:

- Being at least 18 years old.
- Being of sound mind.
- Making your Will in writing.
- Signing the document.
- Having the document signed by two competent adult witnesses.

However, meeting the basic legal requirements is not enough to ensure your Will does what you want it to do. An effective Will is one that not only meets state requirements, but also one that is matched to your needs and desires.

Trusts

These are popular estate planning tools, and one of the least understood. A trust is like a small corporation in that it exists as a legal entity apart from the person who creates it. Trusts can own property like a corporation and are run by people who do not own that property, but who simply manage it or look after it on the trust's behalf. While there are numerous kinds of trusts that you can include in your estate plan, one of the main benefits of using a trust is as an inheritance vehicle. Unlike wills, trust's do not have to go through the probate process. For example, a revocable living trust (also known as an inter-vivo trust, or just a living trust) allows you to make inheritance choices without submitting those choices to a probate court. The probate process is open to public inspection, and is often expensive and time-consuming, which is why revocable living trusts can be so useful.

Transfer-on-Death Assets

A transfer-on-death asset (sometimes known as payable-on-death asset), is an estate planning and inheritance tool. A transfer-on-death asset is automatically inherited by your chosen beneficiary following your demise. With this tool you do not need to make a WILL or a trust to choose who inherits transfer-on-death assets. You simply need to make sure you choose your beneficiary in the manner required under the asset's rules.

WHAT DOES ESTATE PLANNING CONSIST OF?

To understand what an estate is, and its planning, you must know specific definitions and their functions.

- **Estate** - many people struggle with the term **'estate'** with the idea of a large home or property, but that is not what an estate is. It is whatever a person leaves behind after death. Some people might leave a lot, while others might leave behind less. But everyone, no matter who they are, how much they own, or where they live, will leave behind an estate.

- **Probate** - because everyone leaves behind an estate, all states have adopted laws that determine what happens to these items. While laws differ from state to state, they are fundamentally the same, and allow for an efficient and uniform transfer of estate property to new owners. These are known as probate laws, or the probate code. Probate laws protect your right to make decisions about what you want to happen to your estate, but they also require you to make choices through specifically recognized methods, such as by making a Last Will and Testament that complies with all applicable requirements.

- **Estate Plans** - a collection of legally enforceable tools that allows individuals to control what happens to their estates after death. Some estate plans include a small number of tools (a Will, or a Will with a Testamentary Trust), while others are more complicated.

- **Intestacy** - because people are reluctant to think about death, they never create an estate plan. People who die without leaving behind a plan are referred to as **having died intestate.** Because of this, all states have adopted laws that predetermine what happens to these estates. These laws are known as **laws of intestacy, or intestate succession.** Should you die without a plan of your own, your states laws will automatically apply to your estate. Further, you have no control over what these laws choose for you, unless you override them with an estate plan of your own.

Estate Planning Trusts

The following trust types are used in typical estate planning cases, and for which more complicated trusts are based:

- **Revocable Living Trust or Inter Vivo Trust** - this trust, is often established to avoid the probate process, and make sure that assets go to the **trust grantors** (creator) intended recipients without a lengthy court process after the grantor's death. Typically, the revocable living trust is the **'mothership'** containing many sub-trusts.

- **Grantor Trust** - this is the individual who has initiated the trust to transfer property to another person or business entity for purposes of avoiding probate, taxes, or other complications stemming from the disposal of assets.

- **Irrevocable Living Trust** - these trusts are contracts created to transfer or manage assets of an individual that the trust creator claims are not competent to manage property or other assets. The irrevocable aspect can be limited to a portion of the trust, so other parts of the trust could be changed. So, depending on the terms of these trusts, the trusts cannot be changed or reversed.

- **Testamentary Trust** - this trust is created through explicit instructions in the Will of a deceased individual. This type of **'irrevocable trust**' is used to leave assets to a beneficiary but only at a specified time and takes effect upon the grantor's death. This trust does not avoid probate but needs probate to take effect.

- **Minor's Trust** - a trust that passes assets to a child and provides for management of those assets until the child reaches an age that the trust creator specifies, when he or she assumes full control of the assets. Using this type of trust avoids expensive guardianship proceedings needed to manage the assets the child inherits before he or she turns 18 years old. This arrangement holds all assets in the trust secure for the minor child, since the grantor receives no income from the trust's assets.

- **Beneficiary's Trust / Separate Share Trust or Spendthrift Trust** - these trusts allow trustees to manage the assets in a trust for the welfare of the recipient of the trust. Separate **Share Trusts** allow the parents to establish a trust with separate features to accommodate the unique needs of each child, while a **Spendthrift Trust,** or a **trust with a**

spendthrift clause, protects the trust's assets from being claimed by creditors and allows the assets to be managed by an independent trustee.

- **Blind Trust** - this trust allows the trustees or anyone who is holding power of attorney to handle the assets of the trust without the knowledge of the beneficiaries. These trusts can be useful in situations where the beneficiary should be kept unaware of the contents of the trust to avoid conflicts of interest.

- **Discretionary Trust** - with a discretionary trust the beneficiaries and assets are not fixed, but determined by criteria established in the trust instrument and administered at the discretion of the trustees, who will decide which beneficiaries, and which assets from the trust, will be involved.

Elder Care Planning Trusts
These trusts are used to protect assets from expensive long-term care costs:

- **First Party Special Needs Trust (Supplemental Needs Trust)** - a trust established by a family member, guardian, or the court. This trust helps to preserve financial security for individuals with special needs by allowing an individual to benefit from supplemental resources while keeping eligibility for public aid (SSI / Medicaid).

- **Third Party Special Needs Trust (Supplemental Needs Trust)** - this trusts benefits individuals with special needs and is intended to hold assets given or bequeathed to such an individual from a third party (parents or other family members), and provides for the person's care and comfort after using up government benefits. Without this trust, special needs individuals that receive financially based government benefits may lose those benefits.

- **Medicaid Trust (Income Only Trust)** - helps seniors avoid tax issues and probate problems when a spouse living in a nursing home dies. This trust protects assets when an individual has too many resources to be eligible for Medicaid.

- **Pooled Trust** - designed to help disabled people qualify for Medicaid. A pooled trust is run by a nonprofit organization and allows individuals to deposit excess assets (over the Medicare eligibility limits) into the trust, which pays the disabled person's additional bills and allows them to qualify for Medicaid for nursing home benefits.

- **Qualified Income Trust (Miller Trust or QIT)** - protects assets when an individual applying for **Medicaid** has income that exceeds the threshold stated for Medicaid eligibility. The **QIT is an Irrevocable Trust** that creates eligibility for long term nursing home care through Medicaid.

- **Spousal Testamentary Special Needs Trust** - protects assets for the surviving spouse from being absorbed by Medicaid. It is embedded into a will as a **Testamentary Trust** and becomes active upon the death of the grantor, so that the surviving spouse is not considered to be the actual owner of the assets named in the **Trust.**

- **VA Eligibility Trust** - the VA Eligibility Trust protects assets outside the assets limits for long term assisted living, in-home, or nursing care and ensures eligibility for that care if needed.

Estate Tax Planning Trusts

The following trusts are used typically to avoid or reduce income and estate taxes:

- **Credit Shelter Trust** - allows a married person to avoid estate taxes by allowing the assets specified in the trust agreement to be transferred to the beneficiaries, usually the investor's children. This trust allows each spouse to maximize their personal estate tax exemption.

- **Generation Skipping Trust** - places assets in a trust designed to transfer them to a grantor's grandchildren, rather than children, to avoid estate taxes that occur if the deceased's children directly inherit the assets.

- **Grantor Retained Annuity Trust (GRAT)** - allows an individual to make large financial gifts to family members while avoiding the gift tax. The trust is set up as an annuity, allowing the donor to donate and receive an annual payment from the annuity for a fixed term. At the end of the term, remaining assets in the trust go to the beneficiary as a gift.

- **Grantor Retained Unitrust (GRUT)** - this type of irrevocable trust allows the grantor to put assets into the trust and receive a variable amount of income from an annuity during the term of the trust, which can be fixed or for the life of the grantor.

- **Grantor Retained Income Trust (GRIT)** - this type of trust allows the grantor to place assets in the trust for a beneficiary, but still retain the right to receive income from these assets for a certain period of time, after which the beneficiary starts to receive income.

- **Intentionally Defective Grantor Trust** - a trust created to freeze some of an individual's assets for estate tax purposes, the intentionally defective trust is established as a grantor trust with a flaw intentionally built in to ensure that the individual must continue to pay income taxes, which reduces the value of the grantor's estate and allows beneficiaries such as children or grandchildren to receive the full value of the assets.

- **Marital Trust** - creates a trust to benefit a surviving spouse and the heirs of the couple. Assets are moved into the trust when the first spouse dies, and the income generated by the assets are transferred to the surviving spouse. When that individual dies, the remaining assets go to the couple's heirs.

- **QTIP Trust** - provides for a surviving spouse, while allowing the grantor to retain control of the distribution of the trust's assets after the death of the surviving spouse. This type of trust is beneficial for second marriage families and for families wanting to protect assets from predatory marriages.

- **Qualified Personal Residence Trust** - transfers the grantor's residence out of the estate, thereby removing it from the value of the grantor's estate as a gift. Under the terms of the trust, the grantor can continue to live in the residence for a specified number of years rent free, before the beneficiaries of the trust are vested in their interests.

- **Charitable Remainder Annuity Trust (CRAT)** - allows a donor to place a large gift of assets like cash or property into a trust that pays back a fixed amount each year. Upon the donor's death, the remaining assets are transferred to the designated charity.

- **Charitable Lead Annuity Trust (CLAT)** - provides an interest income to a charitable organization, while passing assets to other beneficiaries. Part of this interest goes to another beneficiary, such as the donor, their family members, or other individuals.

- **Charitable Remainder Unitrust (CRUT)** - this irrevocable trust was created under the authority of the Internal Revenue Service and distributes a fixed percentage of its assets to a beneficiary, and at the end of a fixed term, the remainder of the assets are transferred to a designated charitable organization.

- **Charitable Lead Unitrust (CLUT)** - this trust allows a donor to give a variable amount annually from the trust to charity for a fixed term of the life of an individual. When the term of the trust is over, remaining assets are distributed back to the donor or other designated recipient.

- **Sharkfin Charitable Lead Annuity Trust** – this trust allows for small payments to be made into a charitable lead annuity trust for the first few years of the trust term, but a very large payment must be made into the trust in the last year or two.

- **Irrevocable Life Insurance Trust (ILIT)** - this trust helps to preserve the proceeds of life insurance from taxation and allows the Trust to invest a deceased person's life insurance benefit and administer the trust for a surviving spouse and children.

- **Buildup Equity Retirement Trust** - in this trust, a spouse (the donor) makes gifts to the other spouse (the Donee) using an annual gifting exemption instead of an unlimited marital deduction. In this way the assets are exempt from both gift and estate taxes.

THE IRA TRUST

If you have substantial assets in an IRA, you should **consider setting up a special type of revocable living trust that is designed to be the beneficiary of your IRA after you die.** The IRA Trust is referred to by several different names **(IRA Living Trust, IRA Inheritor's Trust, IRA Stretch Trust, IRA Inheritance Trust, and Standalone Retirement Trust),** and has many benefits for your beneficiaries.

Asset and Other Protection for Your Beneficiaries

In general, IRAs are protected from the claims of creditors regarding the **IRA account owner** while he or she is living. However, once the IRA account owner dies and the IRA assets get into the hands of an individual beneficiary, the IRA assets will lose their protected status (see SCOTUS Decision Makes Inherited IRAs Vulnerable to Creditors' Claims for more information).

On the other hand, **IRA assets passing into a sub-trust created for the benefit of an individual beneficiary under the terms of an IRA Trust will be protected from creditors, predators, lawsuits and divorcing spouses if the funds remain inside of the trust and can only be distributed at the discretion of the trustee.** This will ensure that the IRA assets will remain intact for the use and benefit of the beneficiary in the event the beneficiary files for bankruptcy, gets sued, or gets married and then divorced.

- An IRA Trust will protect the beneficiary from his or her own bad decisions, excessive spending habits, inexperience with investing, and overreaching spouses.

    - If your IRA passes to your beneficiaries through an IRA Trust, you can put restrictions on how your IRA assets are spent, when and how much the beneficiary can withdraw. This will create an ongoing legacy for your family since the IRA assets that are not used during a beneficiary's lifetime can continue in trust for the benefit of the beneficiary's descendants. This is important if the beneficiary already has a taxable estate since the IRA Trust can be drafted to minimize, or even eliminate estate taxes in the beneficiary's estate through generation-skipping trust planning.

- An IRA sub-trust created for the beneficiary can be specifically designed as a special needs trust that will ensure the beneficiary continues to receive government assistance.

IRA Hitches

- If your IRA is left directly to your beneficiaries outside of a trust, then your beneficiaries can immediately cash out the IRA, and spend the money as they see fit. If a beneficiary chooses this option 100-percent of the amount withdrawn will be included in the beneficiary's taxable income in the year of withdrawal.

- A different type of problem can be created if you name your minor grandchild as the direct beneficiary of your IRA. If this is the case, a guardianship or conservatorship will need to be established to manage the IRA for the benefit of the grandchild until he or she reaches the age of 18. Then, once the grandchild reaches 18, he or she can withdraw 100-percent of what is left in the IRA without any strings attached.

Planning for a Blended Family

If you are in a second or later marriage, you and your spouse have a blended family. Your IRA Trust can be designed to give your Trustee access to your IRA for the benefit of your spouse during his or her lifetime, but after your spouse dies you can dictate that what is left in the IRA Trust will go to the beneficiaries of your choice. This will keep your IRA out of the hands of your spouse's family, or a new spouse if your spouse chooses to remarry.

MORE TRUSTS?

Although not as popular or used as frequently as other types of trust, we have included the following to be as thorough as possible.

- **Domestic Asset Protection Trust (DAPT)** – are created in states that have anti-creditor trust acts (Alaska, Delaware, South Dakota, Nevada and some others). It allows an individual to establish a trust for his or her own assets that offers protection from creditors.

- **Offshore Asset Protection Trust** - considered the strongest asset protection strategy available, this trust is established in a non-domestic jurisdiction and allow assets to be conveyed to the offshore trusts for protection from seizure in judgments for creditors.

- **Totten Trust** - allows an individual to put money into a bank account or other form of security to be held until death, whereupon the contents of the account will pass to a designated beneficiary without needing to deal with probate. This is also known as a pay on death designation.

- **Land Trust or Illinois Land Trust** - these trusts appoint a trustee to maintain ownership and management of a parcel of real property for the benefit of a beneficiary. These trusts may also be held by nonprofit entities for conservation purposes, or by corporations to accumulate large amounts of land.

- **Gun Trust** - allows the maker to acquire Class 3 weapons and other destructive devices. This trust allows for the transfer of property to and from the trust, and for the modification of trustees and beneficiaries.

CHAPTER 3   PLANNING FOR INCAPACITIES

PLANNING FOR INCAPACITIES

Estate plans are flexible, they do not just protect your interests after you die, but they also protect you if you lose your ability to care for yourself or manage your own assets.

Many adults are physically and mentally capable of making their own choices, but that can change. People who have significant disabilities, those who have been injured, or those who are suffering from the effects of terminal or serious medical conditions often cannot make their own decisions.

Powers of Attorney and Medical Directives

Just as an estate plan allows you to control what happens to your property after you die, it also allows you to protect yourself in the event you lose capacity.

- **Financial Powers of Attorney** - this is a document through which you (the principal) give a legal representative (the agent) of your choosing the authority to make decisions for you. There are many ways you can use powers of attorney, but one of the most common is to name an agent who will manage your financial affairs should you lose capacity. These powers are often referred to as springing powers because they only give your agent decision-making abilities when you become incapacitated.

- **Medical Powers of Attorney** - are designed to give your agent the ability to make healthcare choices for you should you become incapacitated. An agent under a medical power of attorney can discuss your medical history and treatment options with your doctors, accept or refuse medical care on your behalf, or seek opinions from other healthcare providers.

- **Durable Powers of Attorney** – this allows your agent to continue to represent you even after you become incapacitated. Durable powers are essential for incapacity plans, but they are not the only type of powers available. Non-durable Powers of Attorney automatically terminate if you, the principal, lose capacity. These non-durable types of powers of attorney are often used, for example, by people who hire a real estate agent or stock broker, but who do not want that agent to act on their behalf should the principal become incapacitated. For incapacity planning purposes, durable powers of attorney are essential.

Advance Medical Directives

Medical powers of attorney are sometimes referred to as advance or medical directives, though there are many types of advance directives available. An advance medical directive is a document that contains or lists your medical wishes. Should you lose your ability to make choices or communicate your wishes to your healthcare providers, your advance medical directives will serve as your voice.

Advance directives (so named because you make them in advance) include such documents as:

- **Living Will** - a document that states which kinds of healthcare treatments you wish to refuse or accept.

- **Healthcare Proxy** - another term for a healthcare power of attorney, this is a document that states who has the power to make medical choices for you should you become incapacitated.

- **Do-Not-Resuscitate Order (DNR)** - a document that tells your healthcare providers that you do not wish to receive resuscitative treatments, such as cardiopulmonary resuscitation (CPR), in the event your heart or lungs cease functioning.

CHAPTER 4 SELECTING YOUR ATTORNEY

BUYER BEWARE

Estate planning can be difficult to think about. Overall, it forces individuals to contemplate fiscal matters that will occur while they are living and after their own deaths. It is extremely important to ensure that your assets are managed prudently, and that next generational family members will receive inheritances, without incident.

Although any lawyer can draw up a simple will for straightforward situations, experienced **Trust and Estate Planning Attorneys** are more prudent in navigating complicated situations.

The old Latin saying, **"Caveat Emptor,"** or **"Buyer Beware,"** applies to estate planning. If you believe that you will be saving money by using forms found on the Internet, or in a do-it-yourself book to prepare your estate planning documents, then your family will be in for a rude awakening when they learn that part or all of your **Will, Trust, Medical or Financial Power Of Attorney** is not legally valid, or will not work as expected.

The Following is a Brief Guide to Help You in Your Selection,

It Is Not Inclusive!

Estate Planning Tips

When building your estate plan, you may have a variety of concerns. Depending on assets, this may include but not be limited to the following:

- Maintenance of an orderly administration of assets during your life.
- Management of estate assets during your life.
- Reviewing estates involving tenants in common or community property.
- Considerations for assets in multiple states.
- Examining all business assets.
- Naming your children's legal guardians.
- Ensuring that your heirs and loved ones receive your assets.
- Helping to reduce or avoid conflicts and confusion of distributions.
- Minimizing legal expenses and taxes.
- Assessing wealth preservation.

The above topic areas and the questions below, are a good place to start when searching for the best attorney for your needs.

Questions for A Potential Trust and Estate Planning Attorney

The following questions will help you to determine if a prospective attorney is right for you:

- **How long have you been practicing?** - obviously, you should strive to find the most experienced attorney possible. An attorney who has faced challenges from **Probate Courts** or the **Internal Revenue Service (IRS)** and who will know how to overcome confronted hurdles.

- **Does the attorney execute the plan?** - some attorneys merely draw up estate-planning documents, while others also execute the associated trusts. It is more efficient to retain a lawyer in the latter category, who can ensure that the correct assets are transferred into the trust.

- **What other issues does the attorney address?** - as life expectancy increases, so does the probability of long-term physical and mental health issues. Do you help your clients fiscally prepare for the possibility of disability or dementia by drawing up powers of attorney, healthcare directives, and living wills?

- **Does the attorney conduct periodic reviews?** - some estate-planning attorneys will semi-annually or annually review your affairs. This can be important, as adjustments to your plan may be necessary if you experience a life change or a change in your finances. New legislative amendments also could potentially change aspects of your estate planning.

- **Can the attorney create a comprehensive estate plan that includes wills, trusts, and life insurance?** - it is important that your estate attorney can convey the nuances of each estate-planning tool and discern the ones that might be right for you.

- **Do you send all documentation for me to review?** - even though you are working with a skilled estate-planning attorney, it is essential to review all documents and forms to avoid any miscommunication. In addition to the forementioned, inquire if they have any problems with input from other professionals (accountants, money managers, etc.) that are a part of your team. Be clear about what can be modified later, and what is irrevocable before attesting to the documents.

- **How do you charge?** - many attorneys charge flat fees, instead of billing by the hour. Some do both, where they charge a fixed rate for basic services, then charge an hourly rate for special tasks. In any case, it is prudent to inquire about compensation ahead of time to avoid surprises.

- **Is there anyone else in your office, with whom I can discuss issues in your absence?** – although most **Trust and Estate Planning Attorneys** try to make themselves available to their clients, it is important to know that an associate or paralegal will be available to answer questions in an emergency if they are not available.

APPENDIX - A

Glossary

Agent	One who acts for and with authority from another called the principal.
Appraiser	An individual qualified by education, training and experience who is hired to estimate the value of real property based on experience, judgement, facts, and the use of formal appraisal processes.
Beneficiary	A person or persons named in a legal document to inherit money, property, or asset. Wills, trusts, and insurance policies commonly name beneficiaries. Beneficiaries can also be named for 'payable-on-death' accounts.
Bequeath	To leave for another at one's death; another word for 'give.'
Bequest	A gift of an item of personal property (that is anything but real estate) made at death.
Bond	A kind of insurance policy that protects inheritors against loss that the personal representative of an estate (the administrator or executor) might cause.
Codicil	If you wish to make a change or addition to your will, you can add a codicil to it. This amendment keeps the original will in place but adds or changes some terms.
Custodian	The person named to manage property inherited by a minor, under a law called the Uniform Transfers to Minors Act, which has been adopted in most states.
Devisee	Someone who inherits real estate through a will.
Executor	The person named in a will and appointed by the probate court after the will-maker's death, to wind up the affairs of a deceased person.
Failed or Lapsed Gift	A gift made in a will that cannot be given to the intended recipient because that person has not survived the will-maker, and the will does not state what should happen to the gift.
Fiduciary	A person or organization that acts on behalf of another person or persons, putting their clients' interest ahead of their own, with a duty to preserve good faith and trust. Being a fiduciary requires being bound both legally and ethically to act in the other's best interests.
Gift and Estate Tax	A tax imposed on large transfers of property (during life or at death) by the federal government. Some states have their

	own estate taxes as well.
Grantor	Someone who creates a trust; a settlor.
Guardian	If you have minor children, you can name a guardian who will be legally responsible for their care after your death.
Heir	Someone who inherits property under state law if there is no valid will.
Intestate	A person who dies without a will is intestate. State intestacy laws will then decide who your heirs are.
Irrevocable Trust	An irrevocable trust cannot be changed or altered by the settlor.
Issue	Direct descendants, including children, grandchildren, and so on. A spouse, brothers, sisters, parents, and other relatives are not issue.
Legacy	A gift of personal property left at death.
Living Trust	This is an important way to plan for the management of your assets in the future.
Mortgage	A legal document that pledges a property to the lender as security for payment of a debt. The mortgage is a lien on the property. Instead of mortgages, some states use First Trust Deeds.
Personal Property	Any kind of asset except real property.
Per stirpes	A term stipulating that should a beneficiary predecease the testator (the person who has made out the will), the beneficiary's share of the inheritance goes to his or her heirs.
Probate	The legal process through which a court examines, approves, and enacts the terms of a will is known as probate. The process takes several months and includes court fees.
Property Taxes	Taxes paid to state and local governments on the property that is owned.
Real Property	Land and appurtenances including anything of a permanent nature such as structures, trees, minerals, and the interest, benefits, and inherent rights thereof.
Residue or Residuary Estate	All property subject to a will that is not given away specifically in the will. Often, a will leaves certain valuable items to named beneficiaries and then 'the rest and residue of the estate' to another beneficiary.

Revocable Trust	A trust that the settlor can revoke at any time during his or her lifetime.
Settlor	Someone who creates a trust.
Successor Trustee	Someone who takes over as trustee of a trust if the original trustee can no longer serve.
Testamentary	Having to do with a will.
Testator	Someone who writes and executes (signs) a will.
Trustee	Someone who has legal authority over the assets in a trust.

FYI - CLARIFICATIONS

What is the difference between 'per capita' and 'per stripes?'
Per capita is a much simpler concept than per stirpes; this directive simply states that all members of a specific group will receive an equal share of the estate. What group this is remains up to the estate holder.

What is per capita at each generation distribution?
This is an alternative way of distribution, where heirs of the same generation will each receive the same amount. The estate is divided into equal shares at the generation closest to the deceased with surviving heirs.

Parties To, And Their Functions in The Probate Process

Estate Administrator
The person or entity named by the Probate Court to perform the duties normally fulfilled by the Executor of the Estate. This appointment is due to the decedent not having a Will, or if the executor listed in a Will is deemed incapable by a court. The Estate Administrator is also known as a **'personal representative of the estate.'**
Probate Attorney
Probate Attorneys, also called estate or Trust Attorneys, help Executors of the Estate (or Estate Administrators, if there is no Will) manage the probate process. **They also help with estate planning, such as the drafting of Wills or Trusts; advise on Powers of Attorney; or even serve as an Executor or Estate Administrator.**
Executor
The manager of the decedents' property. In some states, if the executor is female, they are called an executrix. Other states simply use the term personal representative or administrator.
Fiduciary
A person who holds a legal or ethical relationship of trust with one or more parties.
Probate Judge
A Probate Judge is a Civil Court Judge and a state judicial official who oversees all aspects of the **'probate court system.'** Estate matters are the most common cases heard in probate courts. Not all states and counties have probate courts, and in some, they are called Surrogate's Courts. By either name, they cover the same legal issues and the judges assigned to them share the same roles and responsibilities.

APPENDIX - B

Benefits of Creating an Itemized Asset List

Listing your personal assets can be tedious and time-consuming. But despite the aggravation, the effort will pay off if you or your spouse should die, or if you need to make an insurance claim if your home is broken into or destroyed by fire, flood or other natural event.

Personal Information

Before starting your **list**, dedicate a beginning page for personal information about you and your spouse. This page should include but not be limited to the following:

- Full legal names.
- Current address.
- Email accounts.
- Online passwords for bills, accounts, and profiles.
- Social Security Numbers.
- Passport Numbers.
- Location of your Will.
- Contact information for:
    - Your Executor if any, Trust and Estate Planning Attorney, if any.
    - Attorney, Accountant, and Financial Advisor.
- Location of your safety deposit box and number.

Creating Your List

First you must select a record keeping system. To do so, you select a system which is user friendly to enter and update your information. Most people select a spread sheet since it is easy to customize, share, change, and add new information too. Another advantage to a spread sheet is that it can be printed, uploaded into the Cloud, or stored on a thumb drive.

Inventory List

Once you start your inventory, you must include as much information as possible about each physical asset.

- Physical Assets - tangible items such as your home, automobiles, artwork, antiques, jewelry, furnishings, and other items that you can see and feel. The evidence of your ownership of physical assets is documented in legal documents including deeds and titles.

- Liabilities and Obligations List - this includes home, car, personal loans, and credit cards.
- Non-Physical Assets - things that are owned on paper or other entitlements that are predicated on your death. Items listed here could include brokerage accounts, 401(k) plans, IRAs, bank accounts, life insurance policies, long-term care policies, homeowners' policies, auto insurance, disability insurance, and health insurance.

Note: Some items may be difficult to classify since they have elements of multiple categories. Do not worry about making a strict distinction between the categories. Just put the items in the categories that you feel best represent them. It is more important that all items are listed than where they appear on your list.

Keep your information up to date. Just because you made a list, your work is not over. You continually purchase things and change assets, so you need to keep your list up to date. Periodically review your list, adding new assets and deleting any assets no longer in your possession. If you acquire or dispose of a significant asset, amend the list as soon as possible following the event. You should note the details of the transaction, such as the date, parties involved, and your reasons for acquisition or disposal.

Destroy previous lists to avoid confusion, replacing the older list with the amended copy.

AFTERWORD

Thank you for reading

Protecting Your Assets in The Pandemic Age

We hope you enjoyed this Value-Added Strategy Publication

Thank you again valued reader,
and we hope to meet you again on another book.

ABOUT THE AUTHOR

Pierre Mouchette is the Founder and CEO of Real Property Experts LLC. He is a graduate of New York University, with a Master's in Business Administration, a Certificate in Real Estate Law - Fairfield University - CT, Graduate of the Realtors Institute – CT, and held licensing as a Real Estate Broker, and a Mortgage Broker.

Pierre is currently authoring Books, Booklets, How-to-Articles, and Guides in retirement. Pierre has an extensive background in real estate investment, business management and sales, supplemented by decades of hands-on-experience in building systems engineering, development, evaluation, and assorted analytical engineering studies.

Using background knowledge and experience, Pierre launched Real Property Experts in 2013 to help simplify real estate investing by connecting investors through innovative technology. In 2018, Pierre created THE SYNCHRONICITY INVESTOR a real estate website to facilitate providing world-class solutions for real estate investors and investment businesses.

At Real Property Experts, we publish for you! At home, at work, or just taking a break we have the solution for you. Our publications are available in:

- **Paperback.**
- **PDF (Portable Document Format).**
- **EPUB (open standard format).**
- **AZW3 (Amazon Kindle eReader).**
- **IBA (Apple iBooks).**

Yes, we have you covered!

Other Titles of Interest in this Category

SKU	DESCRIPTION
VAP-001	PROBATE – A Complete Guide for Real Estate Investors
VAP-002	Protecting Your Assets in The Pandemic Age
VAP-003	Creating an Itemized Asset List

www.ingramcontent.com/pod-product-compliance
Lightning Source LLC
Chambersburg PA
CBHW080911220526
45466CB00011BA/3547